TOURING PITTSBURGH BY TROLLEY

a pictorial review of the early sixties

by Harold A. Smith

Quadrant Press, Inc.
19 West 44th Street
New York, NY 10036
(212)-819-0822

©1992 by Quadrant Press, Inc.
All rights reserved
Edited by Frederick A. Kramer
ISBN 0-915276-48-8

FOREWORD

The first time I visited Pittsburgh was in December of 1961. At the time, I was in the army and assigned to the exhibit unit at Aberdeen Proving Grounds in Maryland. We built recruiting exhibits and displayed them around the country. We set up shop at the University of Pittsburgh at Forbes Street and Bigelow Boulevard in the Oakland section of Pittsburgh. This was a short walk from Forbes Field, former home of the Pirates, and in an area served by two of Pittsburgh's East End trunk lines. Interestingly, Pittsburghers refer to their city as having North and South Sides, but East and West Ends.

In 1961, Pittsburgh's trolley car network was the largest operating system in the nation. It numbered 41 lines, if you count the cutback routings such as 11-EAST ST., 14-AVALON, and 37-SHANNON. It remained largely untouched by bus substitution and abandonment until the mid-sixties, a full decade after other cities had their large systems dismantled in wholesale lots.

Not only was the Pittsburgh Railways system the largest at that time, but also without a doubt, the most picturesque. The extremely hilly topography challenged the imagination and ingenuity of the route planners. Lines operated parallel to the base of steep cliffs, over high bridges, and up steep grades. The steepest grade was on the 21-FINEVIEW line. It was 12.24%, that is, it rose 12.24 feet in every 100 feet.

Many streets were so narrow that autos had to park with two wheels on the sidewalk in order to clear the trolleys. Many turns were so sharp that the center of the trolley would overhang the sidewalk as the trolley turned the corner. Trolleys often squeezed through places so tight that direct bus substitution was impossible.

These lines were a real challenge to the trolleys that plied them for decades. It certainly proved that the PCC trolley design of the mid-1930s was more than just a pretty face.

Belated interest in the value of light rail systems came too late to save much of this colorful operation. Deteriorating bridges and track and an anti-trolley management doomed many valuable lines whose length of private right of way would be valuable today for modern rail transit.

The only survivors of this far-flung steel octopus are the remnants of two interurban lines, one cut back from Charleroi to Library and the other from Washington to Drake, plus the 49-ARLINGTON-WARRINGTON, a combination of the old 49-BELTZHOOVER and 48-ARLINGTON lines and the 42/38 MOUNT LEBANON-BEECHVIEW line. Much of these remaining lines is being rebuilt into a modern high-speed rail line.

The only remnants of the original country trolley operation to be seen today can be found at the outer ends of the Library and Drake lines and along the right of way between South Hills Junction and Castle Shannon in the Saw Mill Run area.

Come along with me and take a tour of Pittsburgh as it was in the early sixties, as the days of the large system were dwindling down to a precious few.

HAROLD. A. SMITH
Ridgewood, NY
April, 1992

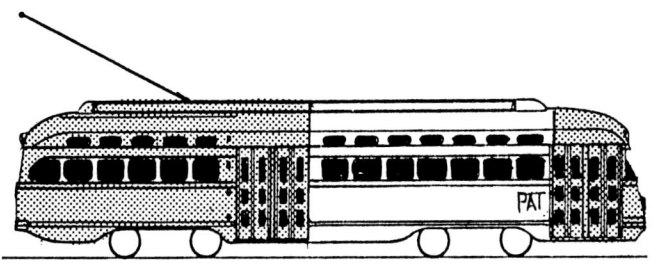

TABLE OF CONTENTS

FOREWORD	2
A BRIEF HISTORY	4
DOWNTOWN	6
THE NORTH SIDE	15
THE EAST END	37
THE SOUTH SIDE	69
RENAISSANCE OF THE SEVENTIES	84
THE ARDEN MUSEUM	88

Photography by the author, except as credited to others.

FRONT COVER:
In an August, 1959 scene reminiscent of the later days of Pittsburgh Railways, No. 1701 heads inbound for the Golden Triangle. The car is turning onto East Street from the Perrysville Avenue trackage that 10-WEST VIEW shared with 8-PERRYSVILLE. *Photograph by Jonathan D. Boyer*

INSIDE FRONT COVER:
Working outbound on 75-WILKINSBURG via EAST LIBERTY, No. 1440 takes the curve at Fifth Avenue and Ross Street. Here in the shadow of the Allegheny County court house, cars on the 22-CROSSTOWN line terminated their runs.

TITLE PAGE:
The cobblestones and single track of Mt. Washington's Southern Avenue greet No. 1672. The car has curved off of Shiloh Street in this June, 1965 view. Next comes the plunge down the steep grade toward double track a few blocks away.

THIS PAGE:
The 48-ARLINGTON line was one of six routes bringing Gimbel's customers downtown via Smithfield Street. Passing Strawberry Street, No. 1664 continues to head for 7th Avenue where it will loop back onto Grant Street for the return trip.

A BRIEF HISTORY

On March 22, 1859 the Citizens Railway Company was formed to operate a horse-drawn street railway car line along Penn Avenue. Its first car ran on August 6, 1859 on a route extending to 34th Street. This route, and all that followed, were built to the "Pennsylvania broad gauge" width of 5 feet, 2-1/2 inches between the rails. As a number of other horse car lines were built, communities such as East Liberty and Aspinwall also received urban transportation.

The next form of urban transport to serve Pittsburgh was the funicular railway, or "inclines" as they are familiarly known in Pittsburgh. The area had 20 such inclines for the movement of passengers and freight up and down the steep hillsides. Sixteen of the inclines carried passengers, and some of these also carried wagons and, later, autos.

While the dates of construction and abandonment of every incline are uncertain, the one with the oldest known opening date is also one of only two still in existence. It is the Monongahela Incline, opened in 1870 and closed for a year in 1983 in order to undergo extensive renovation. Current operation is by the Port Authority Transit. The other surviving incline is the Duquesne incline which opened in 1873. It is still privately operated.

The other passenger inclines were Mount Oliver, Fort Pitt, Penn (17th Street), Saint Clair, Bellevue & Davis Island, Nunnery Hill, Troy Hill, Knoxville, Castle Shannon (which lasted until the 1960s and was the last to carry autos), Castle Shannon South, Clifton, Norwood (Penny), Ridgewood, and Castle Shannon Railroad.

Pittsburgh was among the first cities in the country to attempt the use of electric power to operate street railway service. Early in 1886, the promoters of the Pittsburgh, Knoxville & St. Clair Railway applied to the Daft Company to equip their proposed route on the South Side. It was a formidable routing over grades as steep as 15 per cent. In later years, Pittsburgh Railways route 53 would serve this same area but it would follow a route with somewhat lesser, but still fairly steep, gradients.

The first 800 feet of the 1886 line used conduit collection through a slot in the street. The rest of the line utilized an overhead troller, running on twin contact wires. Cars were pulled by electric locomotives with the first passengers being carried in March of 1888.

Pittsburgh's second electric line ran to the North Side's Observatory Hill using a similar construction. By January 1890, the conduit operation and a rack system used to assist cars on steep grades were discontinued in favor of a more conventional operation. In that same year, the first cars equipped with the Van Depoele system of overhead trolley collector were placed in service, and trolley service was opened along Second Avenue to Glenwood.

While electric rail lines were growing during this period, they were still experimental and primitive. Other cities were finding success with cable-operated lines, and indeed Pittsburgh was to experience the application of this technology as well.

A cable route along 5th Avenue to East Liberty was opened on October 8, 1898. Other cable routes ran on Wylie Avenue and Centre Avenue in the Hill District, and on Butler Street and along Penn Avenue to East Liberty. However, electric railway operation soon proved superior and the cable operations were short lived.

During the 1890s, as many as 190 small companies had formed to provide public transportation with one manner of motive power or another. Many merged and converted to electric operation. The largest mergers produced the Second Avenue Traction, Fort Pitt Traction, Duquesne Traction, and Monongahela Street Railway. These companies were involved in the next wave of consolidations which created the United Traction Company of Pittsburgh, Consolidated Traction Company, and Southern Traction Company.

On December 27, 1901, Southern Traction changed its name to the Pittsburgh Railways Company and entered into operating agreements with the others. At that time, there were 400 miles of single track and 1123 passenger cars, trailers and work cars. There was one exception to this unification of street railway transportation: the Sarah Street line on the South Side. It was the last horse car line, plodding along until 1924 with aging mules and a driver who was nearly 78.

Pittsburgh Railways Company was never a financial success. Its widespread system covered a difficult terrain conquered with expensive construction. Extensive stretches of track to reach the sprawling population produced little revenue. A large number of concessions all requiring payments, had been entered into. And finally, it faced the legal requirement to construct and maintain the road surface for 18 inches beyond its outer rails.

Tragedy struck on Christmas Eve, 1917. Car 4236 ran away downgrade in the South Hills tunnel and overturned at Carson Street, killing 21 and injuring 80. As a result of injury claims, Pittsburgh Railways entered its first bankruptcy and reorganization.

The company emerged from bankruptcy as a property of the Philadelphia Company, a large holding company. This control lasted until 1948, but in 1937, Pittsburgh Railways again slipped into receivership. The company was managed by a board of trustees until 1951 when it was reorganized under its own name and combined with the bus system of the Pittsburgh Motor Coach Company.

Some routes were so unprofitable that they were abandoned in the 1920s, but the system remained basically intact until the reorganization of 1951. Most of the shuttle lines operated by double-end cars were abandoned or converted to feeder bus routes, and the remainder of the system operated by a fleet of 666 PCC cars purchased between 1937 and 1945. This was the nation's largest fleet of these modern streamliners.

The PCC car was a trolley developed by a conference of street railway presidents. The initial letters of President's Conference Committee gave rise to the universally accepted name of PCC to identify that astounding transit vehicle. Fast, attractive, smooth riding, and economical are but a few of the adjectives that describe this bid by the transit industry to improve rail riding and win back business lost to the auto. PCC cars met that objective, particularly so in Pittsburgh.

The first major conversion from trolley service to buses came in 1959. The end of trolley service on all of the West End routes came in one blow when their access to downtown was severed by the closure of the Point bridge. Lines extended north along the Ohio River to Neville Island and as far southwest as Carnegie and Heidelberg.

By the early 1960s, rail service on the outlying routes faced an uncertain future. The Monongahela River towns of McKeesport and Glassport were scheduled to lose their street railway service late in 1963. But before the scheduled date came, a windstorm did in the 98-GLASSPORT line by knocking down the wires. The line was thus abandoned prematurely and, as planned, without a bus replacement. At the extreme eastern end of the system, the 62-TRAFFORD line was abandoned due to poor patronage brought on by the superior service of a parallel bus line.

In 1964, the Port Authority obtained the Pittsburgh Railways Company through condemnation proceedings PAT was bus-minded to a fault. Between 1964 and 1967, it ended trolley service on all North Side and East End lines. By the early 1970s, only the present South Side lines and the 53-CARRICK line remained.

Route 53 did not survive, but subsequent management of PAT saved the rest, upgraded the appearance of the trolleys, and opened a downtown subway that had been dreamed of since 1912. Much of the rest of the system has been converted to a modern light rail line with new cars from Siemens-Duwag in Germany. Projects are under consideration to extend this nucleus of modern public transportation to other parts of greater Pittsburgh.

An interesting bit of technology from the time of Pittsburgh Railways was a device called the headway recorder. The recorders were located at car line terminals, and motormen were required to set the scheduled arrival and departure times on the dials, and press a button to transmit the settings and actual time to the dispatcher's office. Overhead wire contacts at strategic points transmitted the passage of a car. Collectively, these devices enabled a dispatcher to send out a route foreman to check on a delayed car or dispatch extra cars when needed to cover service interruptions. By 1970, this system of timekeeping had declined because operators were reluctant to step out of their vehicles at lonely terminals on late night runs.

DOWNTOWN

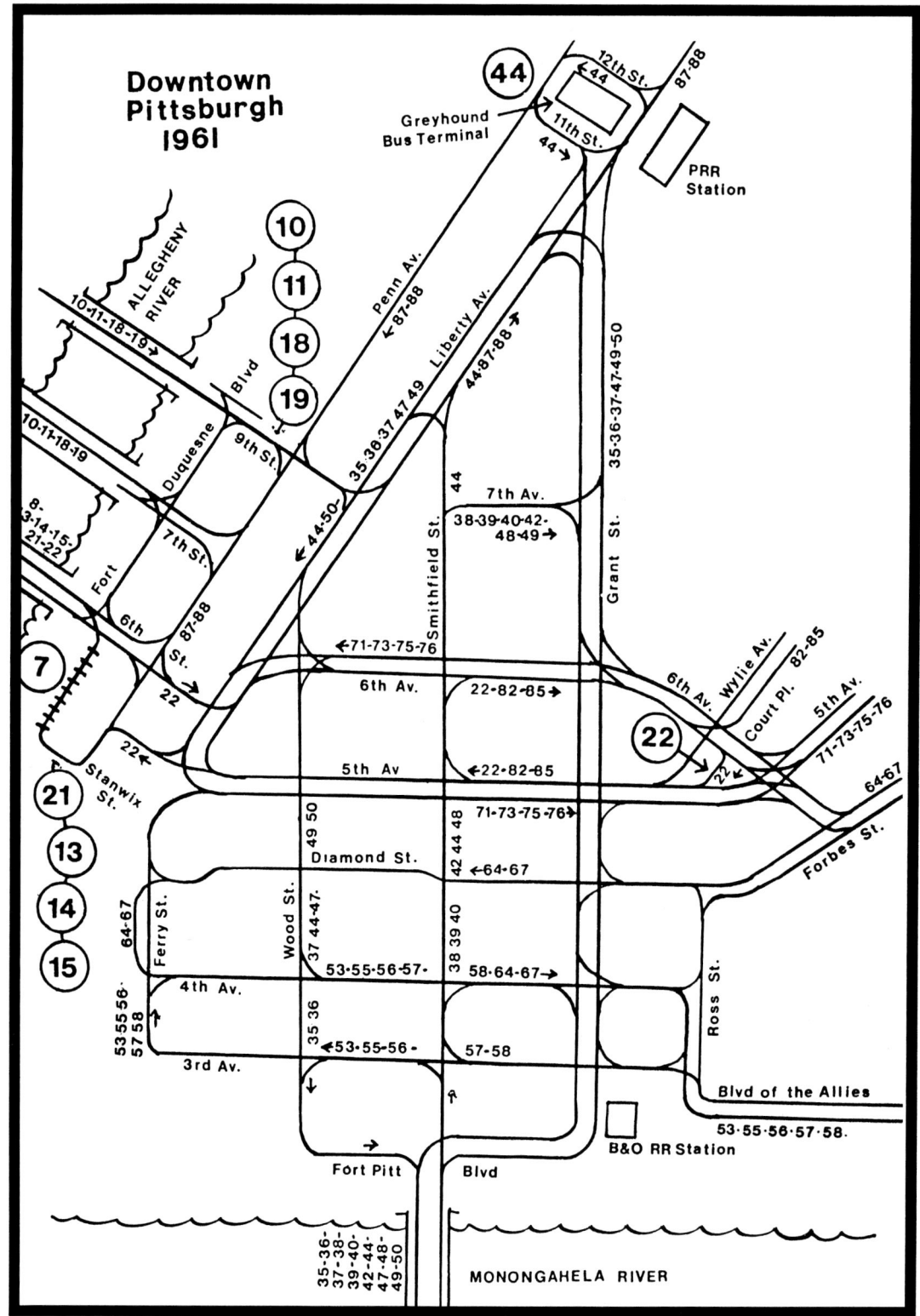

Pittsburgh! The Golden Triangle, historic site of Fort Pitt, the waters of the Allegheny and Monongahela uniting to become the mighty Ohio waterway — Business, financial, educational, recreational, and cultural center of western Pennsylvania — Headquarters city of United States Steel, Alcoa, Gulf Oil, H. J. Heinz, Mellon Bank — Alma Mater to the graduates of the University of Pittsburgh and Carnegie Mellon — Home of the Pirates, Steelers, and Penguins — Focus of a tightly-woven network of public transportation. A metropolis indeed!

There's a first and a last in this picture. The cars seen here are Nos. 1767 and 1797, the first two to be painted in the Port Authority's gray color scheme. This downtown trackage on Fourth Avenue at Cherry Way, between Smithfield and Grant, was among the last to be in service before the subway was opened.

TOP:
In Harm's Way was playing at the Stanley Theater on 7th and Penn Avenues on June 27, 1965, long before its days on late night television. Car No. 1797, working the 8-PERRYSVILLE line, was a post-war model PCC.

BOTTOM:
On Wood Street, No. 1661 carries its passengers south on the 49-BELTZHOOVER line. It is seen crossing Boulevard of the Allies, formerly 2nd Avenue. Pittsburgh is one of the few cities to have radio stations with call letters beginning with both W and K, customarily restricted to eastern and western cities respectively. Pittsburgh's country music station occupies the corner building while the hotel above the trolley is the Sherwyn.

TOP:
No. 1545 on 73-HIGHLAND rolls south on Liberty Avenue at Oliver. One block behind, at Sixth Avenue, is the point where the subway line now turns to run under Liberty Avenue to Gateway Center.

BOTTOM:
The downtown layover point on the 22-CROSSTOWN line was the short block of Court Place between Fifth and Sixth Avenues. A cardboard "PAY ENTER" sign is positioned inside No. 1493's windshield. The trolley wire contactor near the CAR STOP sign will register the car's departure at the dispatcher's office when the car leaves.

9

TOP:
On the other side of the courthouse from the terminal of the 22 line, we find Car 1621 on the 58-GREENFIELD line inbound on Forbes Street. It pauses for traffic at Grant Street.

BOTTOM:
No. 1558, finishing up its inbound run on the 88-FRANKSTOWN line, heads south on Penn Avenue at 10th Street. The Pennsylvania Railroad main line's viaduct is seen in the left background and on the right, the Greyhound Bus Terminal.

Bruce Young

TOP:
A roof headlight marks No. 1700 as one of the PCCs equipped for interurban service. The car has made the transition from Liberty Avenue onto Wood Street signed for SHANNON-DRAKE. In 1964, the building at left housed Azen's Dress Shop. Today it is an entrance for the subway under Sixth Avenue, a half block away.

BOTTOM:
Inbound on 8-PERRYSVILLE, No. 1683 approaches Fort Duquesne Boulevard in May of 1963. This Allegheny River crossing is the Sixth Street Bridge whose deck is suspended from a chain of multiple steel links.

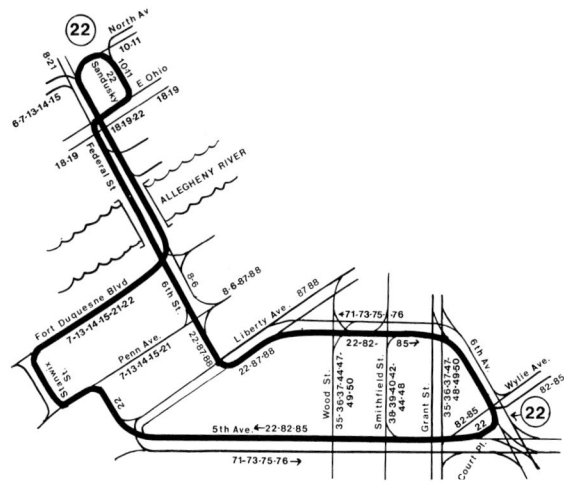

The 22-CROSSTOWN line handled the heavy passenger loads moving within and between the downtown and near North Side areas. Uninteresting to ride, it was a genuine people mover that used the tracks of other trolley lines. Given the location and its looping route, this was the usual assignment for those cars that billboarded paid advertising as well as public service messages for the planetarium, the Red Cross blood drive, safety slogans, and the like.

TOP, RIGHT:
Resplendent in white, light green and dark blue, No. 1560 advertises "inspiring sky dramas" at the Buhl Planetarium. The scene is at Carnegie Hall on East Ohio Avenue in the near North Side on the afternoon of June 8, 1964. Carnegie Hall is one of many cultural institutions and gifts given to the city by the Carnegie Foundation in memory of the Scottish steel magnate who made his fortune in Pittsburgh.

BOTTOM:
No. 1664 was the rolling billboard for Mohawk Airlines. The white, navy blue and gold extravaganza heads east on Federal Street toward the Allegheny River and downtown. The overpass in the background carries the Pennsylvania Railroad's tracks. This area located close to the heart of the city was extensively rebuilt and revitalized through urban renewal. Today there are few of the old landmarks, and it is difficult to trace the exact route of the old car lines.

The official name for the combined routes 77 and 54 was NORTH SIDE-CARRICK via BLOOMFIELD, and it was designated 77/54. Small wonder that the line's nickname was the "Flying Fraction." It takes a map to adequately describe and understand the Flying Fraction's route, as it seemed to meander from North Side to South Side by way of the East End by taking the most indirect of routes. Actually, this Pittsburgh Railways' line had been doing for years what highway planners would come to call beltways or peripheral highways. There always has been a need to serve the flow of traffic generated by people moving crosswise to travel routes radiating out from the center of the city.

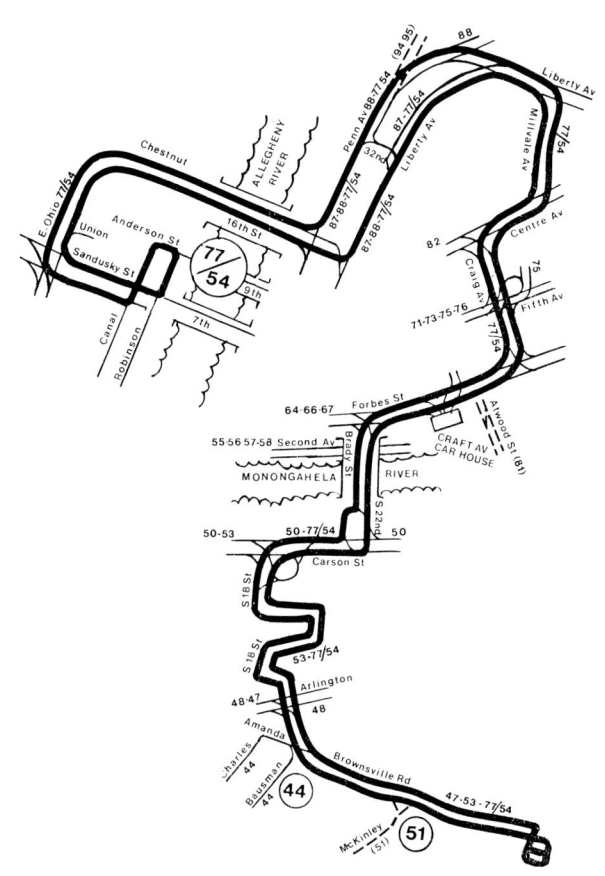

BOTTOM:
By the time this picture of No. 1612 was taken in June of 1964, the route no longer ran through to Carrick, having been cut back to Gist Street on the Oakland side of the Brady Street bridge. The remains of the track switch in the foreground of East Ohio Avenue once connected to the Union Street line.

THE NORTH SIDE

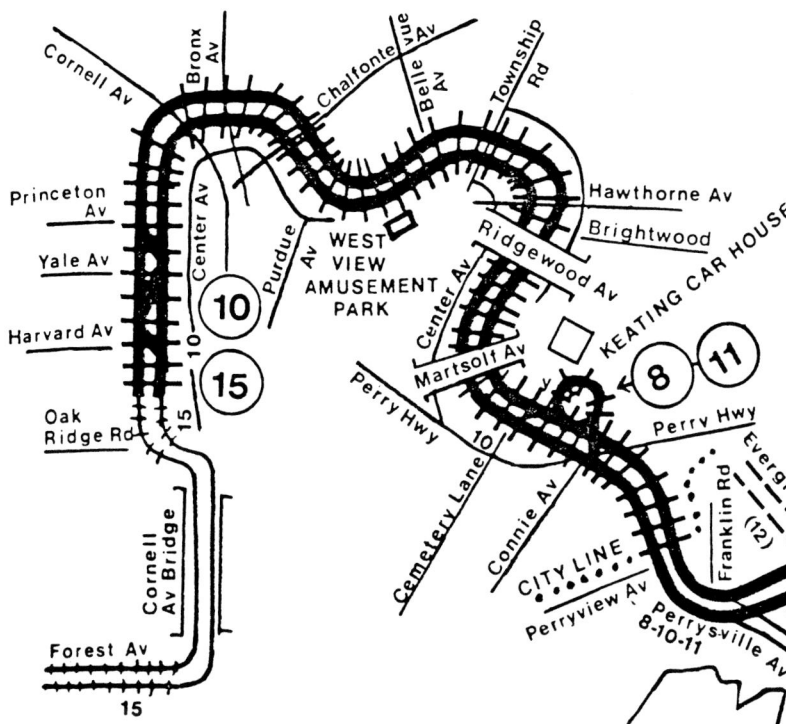

This pictorial review of North Side trolleys begins with the **10-WEST VIEW** and **15-BELLEVUE** lines. Both lines left downtown, headed north across the Allegheny River, and took individual double-track routes routes to the West View area. There was no turning loop at their destination. The double-track lines simply met. Thus, cars outbound on the 10 line continued straight ahead and became inbound route 15 cars. Similarly, outbound 15 cars through-routed to become inbound route 10 cars. Downtown, each route did make a loop so that inbound route 10 cars returned outbound on route 10, and the same for route 15. Operationally, the lines formed an inverted-U with a different route designation on each leg.

OPPOSITE PAGE:
No. 1795 operates inbound on 10-WEST VIEW in June, 1964. Trolleys used a private right of way north of the city line. The section seen here is adjacent to Center Avenue at the Martsolf Avenue overpass.

TOP:
About two miles from downtown, the 10-WEST VIEW line pushes northward, uphill on East Street. This 1964 view of No. 1778 looks back toward downtown from a point near Hazlett Street. The awesome bridge in the background is the East Street bridge, named not for the street it carries but for the street it spans. Built with a 1926 bond issue, the bridge's 220-foot height makes it no place for acrophobes fearful of looking down upon vehicles which appear like toys.

BOTTOM:
No. 1798 reaches the important intersection of East Street with Perrysville Avenue. The Rexall drug store will help in relating this picture with others taken at this junction, including the color picture on the front cover.

TOP:
The **8-PERRYSVILLE** line was named for the avenue of its route, as Perrysville itself is located north of West View, well beyond the trolley system. Route 8 started downtown where route 15 cars loaded, worked diagonally across the near North Side, and reached higher elevation more quickly than 10-WEST VIEW. No. 1797 is seen reaching the East Street intersection on June 8, 1964.

BOTTOM:
Hard times befell local movie theatres when the miracle of television came to everyone's house. The Perry-Harris theatre, despite having two names dear to Pennsylvanians, was dark in 1964 as chartered car No. 1791 breezed by from West View.

TOP, LEFT:
The joint trackage of routes 8 and 10 left the paving of Perrysville Avenue at the city line. No. 1790, which was to become the last car to operate the 10-WEST VIEW/15-BELLEVUE line, makes the short S-turn leading to private right of way.

BOTTOM, LEFT:
The right of way crossed Perry Highway at Connie Drive with trolleys popping up and out onto the highway protected by crossing flashers. The housing development down in the hollow is Ivory Towers, once advertised on a billboard car.

TOP, RIGHT:
This view from across the street shows the steepness of the climb to the Perry Highway crossing. Extreme caution was needed because the highway is US 19, the principal route to Erie in the days before the interstate system was built.

BOTTOM, RIGHT:
The track in the foreground leads into Keating car house, terminus of the 8-PERRYSVILLE line. No. 1780, en route to West View, is delayed by work on the overhead. The crossbuck and flashers can be seen behind the luncheonette's menu sign.

A rain shower on June 8, 1964 gave rise to pools that reflected the overhead wires at Keating car house. No. 1795 is inbound on 10-WEST VIEW and prepares to cross Perry Highway and dive down the right of way toward the city. The car house and its office building were substantial brick structures, with a PITTSBURGH RAILWAYS legend cast in concrete visible above car No. 1790. At this time, all North Side trolley lines worked out of this car house and both the 8-PERRYSVILLE and the route 10 short turn cars carrying 11-EAST STREET destination signs ended their outbound runs here.

TOP:
The double-track right of way to West View continues north, curving along Center Avenue. The tracks duck under two graceful overpasses, the first of which is at Martsolf Avenue. Inbound No. 1784 leans to the curve as it speeds by, the overpass in the background.

BOTTOM:
The second overpass carries Ridgewood Avenue over the tracks near Brightwood Avenue. With streets on both sides of the tracks at this point, No. 1483 finds itself heading inbound on center-of-the-road right of way.

TOP:
Ivory Towers billboard car No. 1605 has reached West View Amusement Park, its roller coaster visible to the left of the car. The nation was once replete with amusement parks reached by trolley cars. Usually the parks were owned by the streetcar company and usually located at the end of a line. West View became the last amusement park in the United States to be served by a trolley line, and today both park and trolley are gone.

BOTTOM:
The same car, upon leaving West View Park, traverses a right of way so weed grown that it looks like a living room carpet.

OPPOSITE PAGE:
The track point where routes 10 and 15 met is here along Center Avenue in West View. No. 1788 thuds across one of three crossovers in the area. This track configuration permitted the route foreman to isolate work equipment or a disabled car, and could be used to establish a holding area for cars awaiting throngs of people at West View Park. But in normal operation, cars breezed by the signal lamps without fanfare. It was the operator's responsibility to turn his destination sign from one route to the other at or near this place.

MAP:
The next pages cover trolleys working 15-BELLEVUE but, as can be seen, route 13-EMSWORTH and its short-turn 14-AVALON shared the trackage over most of the distance to the downtown area. Those lines will be covered after route 15 and will include additional pictures along the shared trackage. Pictorial coverage of other North Side lines shown on this map will follow.

BOTTOM:
Ivy League college names were the theme when streets in this area were developed. No. 1560, the star-studded Buhl Planetarium car, is near Yale Avenue as it closes out its outbound run on 15-BELLEVUE. The vantage point for this picture is the front window of an inbound route 15 car. One of the crossovers can be seen nestled in the weeds.

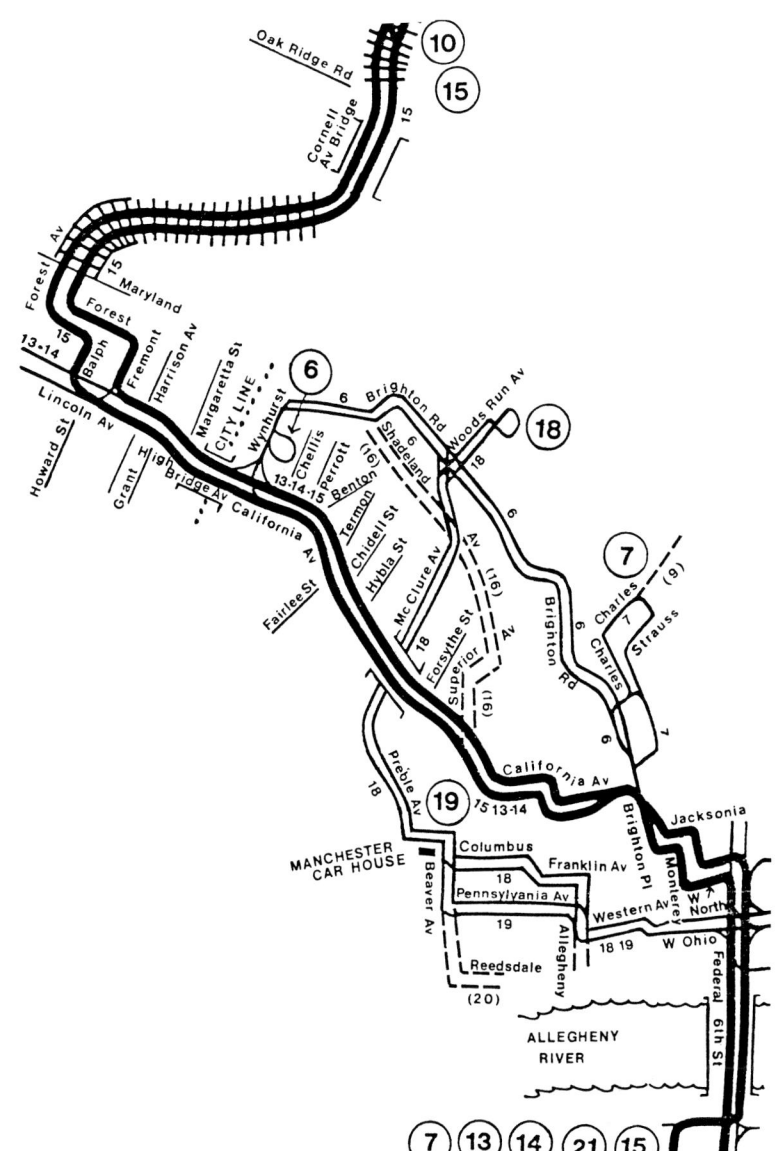

To reach the Bellevue area from the north, Route 15 crossed a deep gorge on a picturesque bit of antiquity, the Cornell Avenue bridge. The timbered floor of this bridge was covered with metal plates and its load limit was nine tons.

TOP:
Inbound cars such as No. 1790 entered the bridge from the center-of-the-road right of way at Oak Ridge Road. Motorists were warned that the railway roadbed was not paved, and later directed to keep right.

MIDDLE:
No. 1798 was outbound off of the bridge on June 8, 1964.

BOTTOM:
Inbound No. 1685 nears the cobblestone apron at the Bellevue end of the Cornell Avenue bridge.

TOP:
On the Bellevue side of the Cornell Avenue bridge, inbound **15-BELLEVUE** cars followed Forest Avenue which, as seen, was an unpaved lane at this point. The railway was, of course, double-tracked and No. 1788 bounced along at speed on its way downtown.

BOTTOM:
Forest Avenue improved as it neared Bellevue center, the tracks occupying a center strip right of way. No. 1798 is within a few feet of the end of private right of way on the line. It will be street running from here on.

TOP:
Outbound No. 1792 turns away from the shops on Lincoln Avenue and pokes its nose up Fremont Street in June of 1964.

MIDDLE:
This bridge on California Avenue spans McClure Avenue. Passengers sitting on the right hand side of No. 1792 can look down below and see the Ohio River and the Western State Penitentiary. The car slows to receive passengers boarding at Forsythe Street.

BOTTOM:
Across the Allegheny River from its downtown destination, No. 1787 passes Buhl Planetarium at Federal Street and East Ohio Avenue.

MAP:
13-EMSWORTH and its short-turn **14-AVALON** originated downtown and shared trackage with route 15 as far as Bellevue. This map section covers the remaining two and half miles to Emsworth, and shows the location of Avalon loop one mile beyond the junction points with route 15.

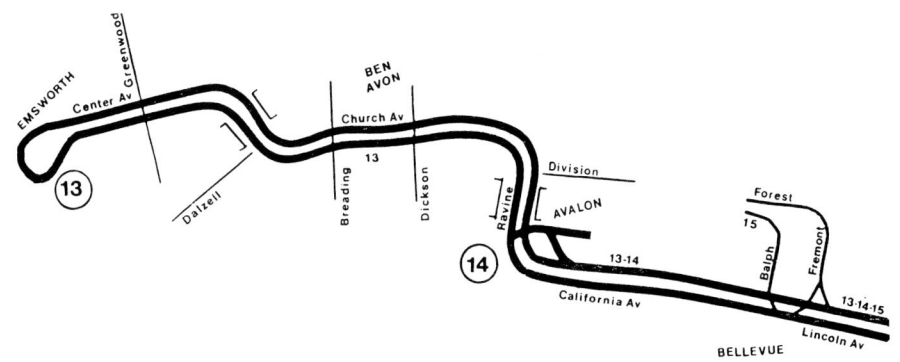

No. 1683 scoots up California Avenue toward Avalon. Large, substantially built Victorian homes with interesting roof lines crowd the block near Fairlee Street.

27

Traffic on Lincoln Avenue in the business district of Bellevue is held up momentarily as No. 1689 pauses at Balph Avenue. The car is working inbound on 13-EMSWORTH. Curved track in the foreground carries inbound route 15 cars to join the long march to downtown Pittsburgh.

TOP:
Carrying a 13-EMSWORTH destination sign, No. 1685 squeals out of the rush hour cutback loop at Avalon. The car is on Ravine Street, curving onto California Avenue. The entire intersection is paved in cobblestone and herringbone pattern brick.

BOTTOM:
Church Avenue carried Route 13 trolleys through the lovely community of Ben Avon, midway between Avalon and Emsworth. No. 1475 drifts past Dickson Street while making a long non-revenue run to Keating car house. However, revenue was derived from advertising which urged hometown fans to follow the Pirates in this 1964 baseball season.

No. 1794 has started the inbound trek from Emsworth. The car squeezes past a line of parked automobiles. The electric power line squeezes past the building with the bay windows by means of alley-arm construction on top of the pole next to the pickup truck. The next pole, seen above the rear of the trolley, has regular crossarm construction.

Trolleys and automobiles shared many bridges to overcome the rough topography of the Pittsburgh area. Some of the bridges were quite old and narrow, not at all suited to the demands of faster and heavier road traffic. 13-EMSWORTH was one of the lines which used such a bridge, replacement of which was ostensibly responsible for cessation of trolley service. Having cleared the bridge, inbound No. 1686 prepares to resume its normal travelling speed.

TOP:
The 7-CHARLES STREET line had only six months to go before abandonment when this scene of No. 1279 at the terminal was recorded on March 27, 1961. In earlier times, the 9-CHARLES STREET TRANSFER line ran from this point up the hill to Charles Street and Perrysville Avenue where it connected with the 21-FINEVIEW line and route 8-PERRYSVILLE. This connection was abandoned on September 14, 1951.

Bruce Young

BOTTOM:
No. 1689, prepared for service on the 6-BRIGHTON ROAD line, completes its deadhead trip from Keating car house as it turns from California Avenue onto Wynhurst. It is June of 1965, and in December of that year, the 6-BRIGHTON ROAD and 13-EMSWORTH lines will be through-routed with the 13 line discontinued between this intersection at Wynhurst Avenue and Brighton Place in the near North Side.

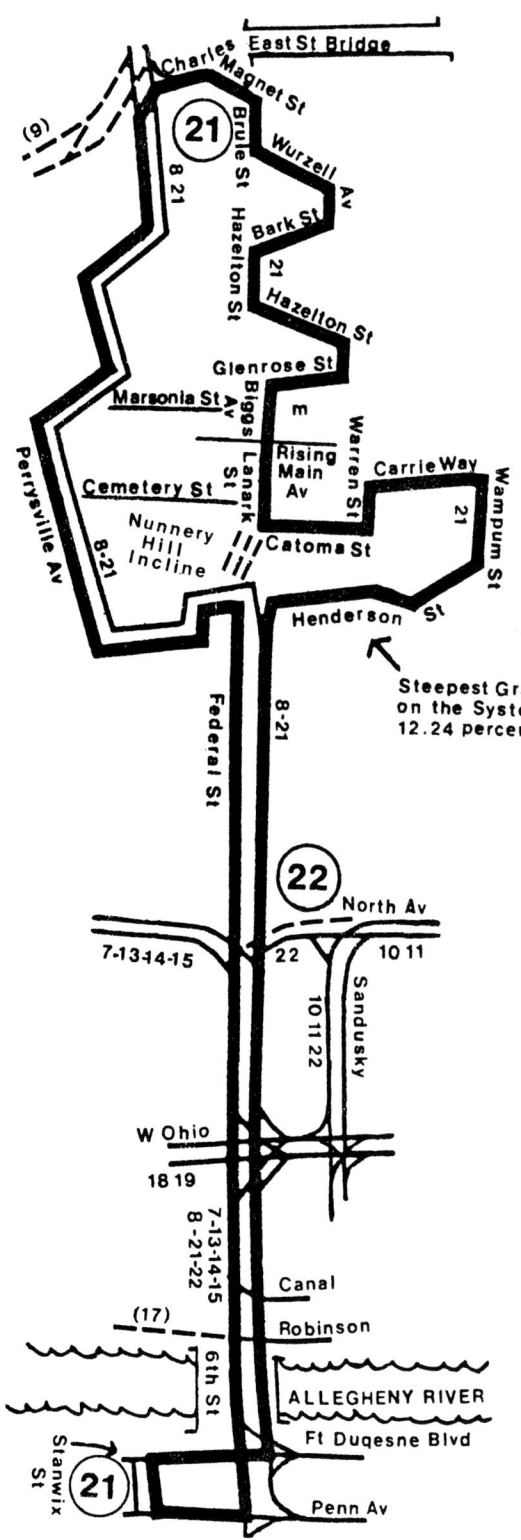

MAP:
21-FINEVIEW was a must on every railfan's Pittsburgh itinerary. Steep and sharp, its tracks squirmed through tight places.

LEFT:
The camera angle deceives, failing to convey the steepness of Lanark Street as No. 1690 scrambles up this narrow alley.

Playing mountain goat as it ascends steep Carrie Way, No. 1690 approaches Warren Street. Because 21-FINEVIEW had the steepest grades on the system, cars assigned to the line were all from a group in the 1600 series which were equipped with special gearing and brakes.

No. 1690 has just discharged two passengers on Catoma Street before turning onto Lanark Avenue. The summit station of the long-abandoned Nunnery Hill incline was located here. Its base station was at Federal and Henderson Streets.

TOP:
A line of shrubs marks the starting edge of a steep drop at the side of Biggs Avenue. No. 1690 hugs the rails above the cliff at the Marsonia Avenue intersection on June 27, 1965, less than a year away from abandonment.

BOTTOM:
With a light dusting of snow on the ground in December of 1961, No. 1686 climbs Bark Street near Wurzell Avenue. Beyond this point, the right of way was just wide enough for a trolley. 21-FINEVIEW was abandoned without a bus replacement. No bus could negotiate the rugged, challenging right of way.

TOP:
Layover point on 21-FINEVIEW was in the middle of traffic at its terminus, Charles Street and Perrysville Avenue. Entrance to the 220-foot high East Street bridge which vaults over route 10 is in the background beyond the overpass.

BOTTOM:
Inbound on 8-PERRYSVILLE, No. 1797 arrives at Charles Street and Perrysville Avenue. The turnoff from the right was used by 21-FINEVIEW cars returning to Keating car house. Disconnected tracks in front of No. 1797 once carried cars on the 9-CHARLES STREET TRANSFER line, abandoned in 1951. The curve in the extreme foreground was the normal track for cars on 21-FINEVIEW as they operated inbound via route 8.

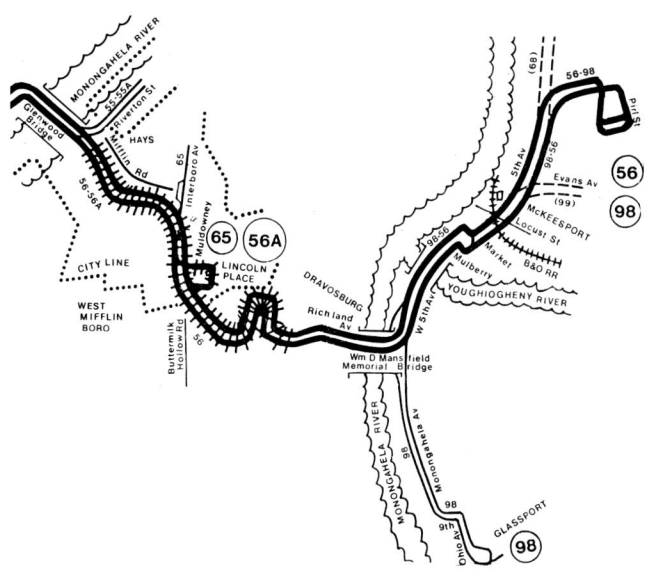

THE EAST END

OPPOSITE PAGE:
Routes 55-HOMESTEAD BRADDOCK EAST PITTSBURGH and 56-McKEESPORT via 2nd AVENUE used the old wooden-planked Glenwood truss bridge to reach the areas of the East End which they served. The bridge crossed the Monongahela River and the Baltimore & Ohio Railroad a little over five miles upstream from the Golden Triangle. In less than a month after this picture was taken in June of 1964, the bridge was closed.

MAP:
The East End lines were spread out over an extensive geographical area. This map covers little more than the outer end of Route 56 and all of 98-GLASSPORT.

BOTTOM:
The McKeesport terminal was at Pirl Street. No. 1741, assigned to a 98-GLASSPORT run, prepares to swing onto the inside track of the two track loop.

TOP:
The central business district of McKeesport stretches along 5th Avenue east of the bridge over the Youghiogheny River. In this busy area, the Baltimore & Ohio Railroad crossed at grade. The crossing gates salute No. 1400 as it thuds across the special work, outbound on 56-McKEESPORT via 2nd AVENUE.

BOTTOM:
Inbound No. 1444 reaches the crossing diamonds in a view that shows the B&O depot. When the Chessie System instituted train service to McKeesport in cooperation with PAT in the 1970s, the station for the new service was at a different location.

TOP:
Bridges in the greater Pittsburgh area are impressive, and this bridge carrying routes 56 and 98 over the Youghiogheny River at McKeesport is no exception. As cars on 98-GLASSPORT pass, No. 1448 is seen leaving McKeesport from the interior of a counterpart entering town.

MIDDLE:
Having crossed the Monogahela, curved off the Mansfield bridge, and sprinted down the ramp into the western reaches of McKeesport, No. 1431 passes a safety island. It is en route to its terminal in the east end of town. The track switch in the right foreground carries route 98 cars beneath the bridge en route to Glassport.

BOTTOM:
No. 1448 streaks across the Mansfield bridge plaza on its way to McKeesport from Glassport. The tracks in the foreground are the 56 line's entry and exit from the bridge.

TOP:
The clean, industrial lines of the Mansfield bridge structure are graced by the soft curves of the PCC car design and the smooth styling of Ford's Thunderbird model. The far end of this spacious river crossing is in Dravosburg.

BOTTOM:
No. 1412, inbound on 56-McKEESPORT via 2nd AVENUE, makes a service stop at Buttermilk Hollow on August 28, 1963. The bus line that replaced trolleys on route 56 didn't follow the private right of way closely. At this point, the nearest stop was a quarter mile away.

Bruce Young

TOP:
By May of 1963, No. 1664 was no longer an advertising car painted for Mohawk Airlines. Operating inbound on the 56-McKEESPORT via 2nd AVENUE line, the car discharges two passengers at Riverton Street. The line's private right of way from Dravosburg ends here where the tracks join those of the 55 line. Just ahead, the car will cross the Monongahela River on the Glenwood bridge and continue toward downtown.

BOTTOM:
The trolley seen against this industrial background on 2nd Avenue is No. 1797. At left, knowledge about the workings of the plant are passed from one generation to another.

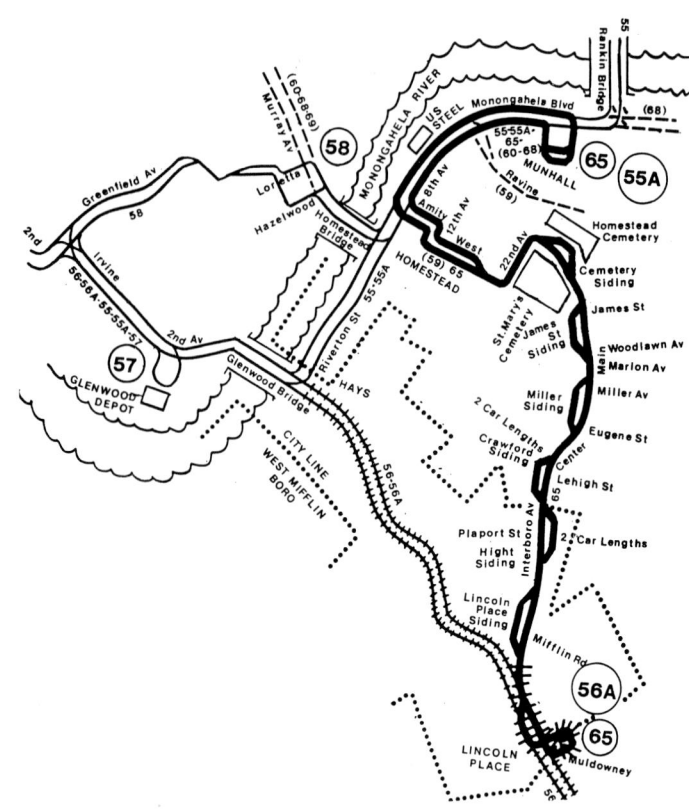

MAP:
By a wide margin, the preponderance of Pittsburgh Railways trolley routes were double tracked. A notable exception was route 65-MUNHALL LINCOLN PLACE which had an abundance of passing sidings along what was basically a single-track line. This interesting operation triangulated between a portion of 56-McKEESPORT via 2nd AVENUE and 55-HOMESTEAD BRADDOCK EAST PITTSBURGH.

BOTTOM:
No. 1412 swings off the 56 line right of way at Interboro Avenue on its way to the Munhall terminal.

This diamond-shaped turnout, a standard fixture on street railways everywhere, was located at Miller Avenue on Main Street. 65-MUNHALL LINCOLN PLACE had six such passing points. Passing sidings were short, as was the distance between them. This allowed a delay on a car moving in one direction to have minimum scheduling impact on a car moving in the opposite direction because the approaching car could move ahead to the next siding under signal protection. No. 1442 is Homestead-bound, and the effect upon automobile traffic of swinging from the center of the street to the right lane can be seen by the line of vehicles behind the trolley.

TOP:
Heading for Munhall, No. 1412 crests the hill at Marion Street on the single track between the James Street and Miller sidings. Virtually all lines in Pittsburgh had a choppy profile, and 65 MUNHALL LINCOLN PLACE was no exception.

BOTTOM:
Caution is the byword for cars turning from Main Street onto 22nd Avenue. The single track on East 22nd Avenue was not centered, evidently the result of a street widening program years earlier. As a result, trolleys bound for Munhall travelled one block on the "wrong side" of the street. St. Mary's Cemetery is on the right.

TOP:
The hustle and bustle on East Eighth Avenue in Homestead surrounds No. 1670. Bound for Lincoln Place, the trolley approaches the safety island at Amity. 65-MUNHALL LINCOLN PLACE turned left at this intersection, leaving the tracks of the 55-HOMESTEAD BRADDOCK EAST PITTSBURGH line.

BOTTOM:
No. 1455, on 65-MUNHALL LINCOLN PLACE, shares the Munhall loop with Mack bus No. 75 operating on the 60-EAST LIBERTY HOMESTEAD line.

Richard Anderson

TOP:
No. 1431 rolls outbound on the 55A-MUNHALL via 2nd AVENUE, a cutback routing of route 55. The car has reached the foot of Second Avenue, taking the curve that leads to the Glenwood bridge. Iron City beer, a local favorite, keeps its name before the public.

BOTTOM:
No. 1641 treads carefully onto the old Glenwood bridge, heading outbound on 55-HOMESTEAD BRADDOCK EAST PITTSBURGH in June of 1964. A year earlier, the 56-McKEESPORT via 2nd AVENUE trolley route had not yet been abandoned and its cars also used the bridge.

TOP:
This view looking toward the bridge on Second Avenue catches No. 1472 inbound on route 55. The inevitable closing of the old Glenwood bridge was foretold by the sign saying "SLOW - TRAVEL AT YOUR OWN RISK." The bridge had not yet been condemned, and it continued to carry the trolleys and traffic on Pennsylvania highway route 885. Perhaps the greatest hazard was damage to automobile tires from possible breakage of strap iron bands which kept the timber flooring from moving.

BOTTOM:
Quite the proper place for a Pittsburgh trolley car to be found was at the United States Steel works at Homestead. No. 1658 points outbound.

TOP:
In common with lengthy routes 55 and 56, the much shorter 58-GREENFIELD line left downtown and headed toward the Glenwood section via Second Avenue. In the industrial area, these routes were sandwiched between the Baltimore & Ohio Railroad and works along the Monongahela River. No. 1448 picks up a passenger on its inbound run.

The end of the 58-GREENFIELD line was at Greenfield and Hazelwood Avenues. The terminus was reached by climbing and twisting up Greenfield Avenue from Second Avenue on a largely single tracked right of way. No. 1631 commands the corner, ready for its return trip downtown on June 9, 1964. Trolley service to the Hazelwood community was to end in less than a month.

TOP:
One of the principal lines serving the East End was 64-EAST PITTSBURGH WILKINSBURG. The line started downtown, ran east on Forbes Avenue through Oakland, circled through Wilkinsburg, turned south through the Edgewood section, and homed in on its destination in East Pittsburgh. About a dozen miles of travel were involved. Two miles from downtown, route 64 passed in front of the Craft Avenue car house where inbound No. 1768 is seen. The safety island featured a modest shelter from the weather and an ornate lamp to warn motorists of this obstruction to their line of travel.

BOTTOM:
The early morning sun of May 19, 1963 shines on outbound No. 1520 at Pennant Place, a tribute to the World Champion 1960 Pirates who defeated the Yankees four games to three. In the shadows lies one of White Tower's hamburger palaces, this one a favorite of motormen picking up coffee as they headed out of Craft Avenue on the first runs of the morning.

OPPOSITE PAGE:
This pleasant residential section of Wilkinsburg is not far from the business district. No. 1767 climbs Kelly Street near Trenton in June of 1965. The varied patterns and tones of brick paving give a substantial feel to the neighborhood.

TOP:
Wide and busy Forbes Street narrows to this cobblestone right of way in Wilkinsburg. The view is at Celeron Street where No. 1753 has just turned from Peebles Street on its way downtown in June of 1965.

BOTTOM:
No. 1734, inbound on 64-EAST PITTSBURGH WILKINSBURG waits in the background while No. 1547 on 76-HAMILTON leaves the Jane Street loop. The cars head north on Coal Street toward the Wilkinsburg business district.

TOP:
Both No. 1765 nearing the end of its run on 64-EAST PITTSBURGH WILKINSBURG line and the 87-ARDMORE car from which this was taken turn onto Electric Avenue in East Pittsburgh. Westinghouse is the major employer in this area, giving rise to street names such as Electric Avenue and Air Brake Avenue. The view down Braddock Avenue finds a number of cars parked over the curb line giving better clearance for traffic.

BOTTOM:
The layover point for route 64 in East Pittsburgh was on Beech Street at Linden. No. 1767 rests with all doors open on June 27, 1965.

Like route 64, route 67-SWISSVALE RANKIN BRADDOCK followed east on busy Forbes Street from downtown, turning southeast just before crossing the city line into Wilkinsburg. Then through Swissvale and Rankin, the line twisted down through the mill area along the Monongahela and ended in a loop at the Carneige-Illinois steel works. No. 1756 pauses on Forbes at Bigelow Boulevard in front of a University of Pittsburgh building in December of 1961. This spot is just the throw of a baseball from Forbes Field.

Pittsburgh Railways placed eight orders for PCC trolleys, all with St. Louis Car Company between March, 1936 and October, 1947. No. 1756 was from the final order and was delivered in early 1948. Unlike earlier model cars, these had an all-electric braking system instead of conventional air brakes. These cars were equipped with ceiling fan ventilation; windows were sealed instead of having a mechanism to open them. Dash lights originally supplied on this series of cars have been removed.

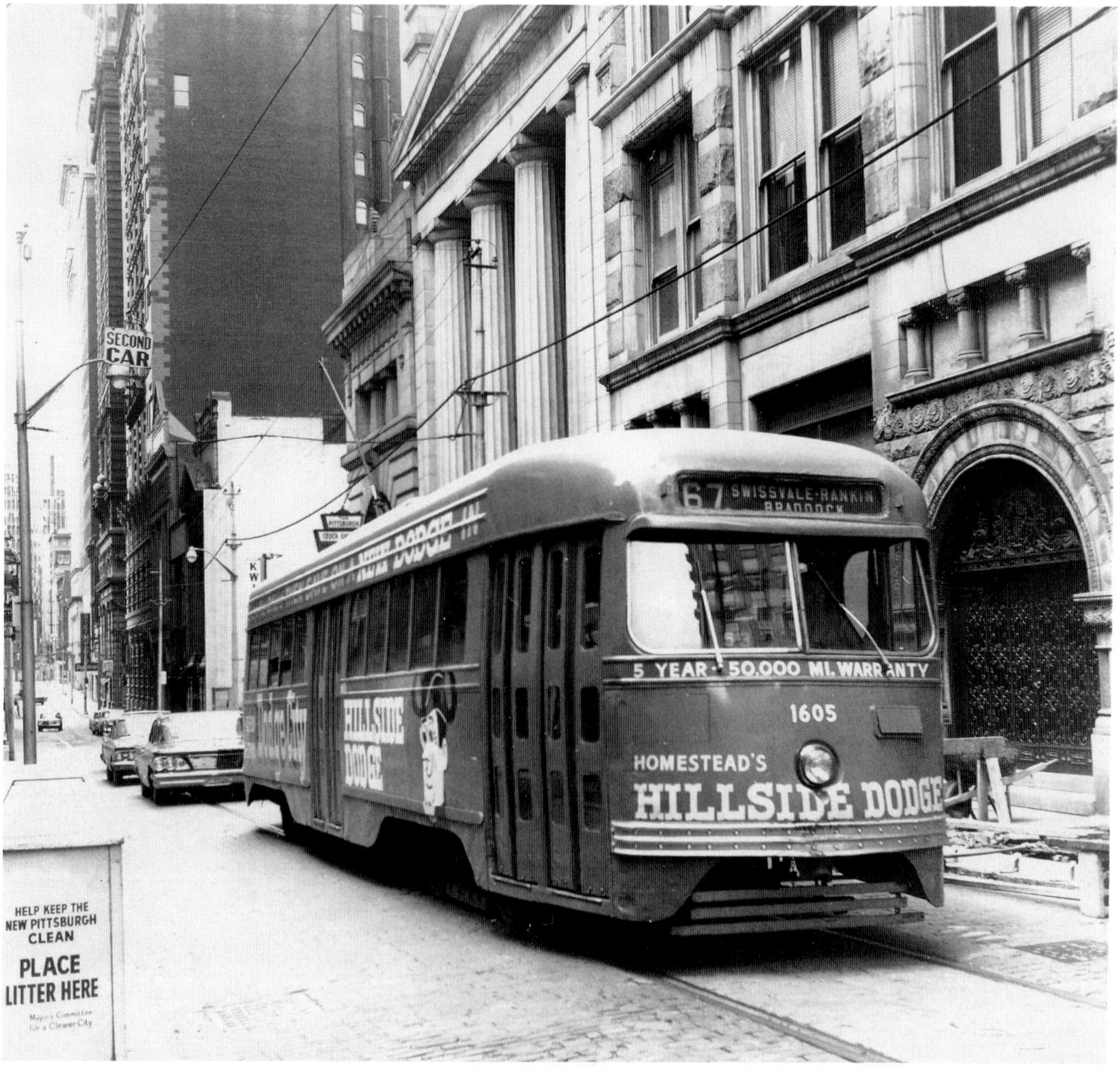
SECOND
CAR
67 SWISSVALE-RANKIN
BRADDOCK
5 YEAR · 50,000 MI. WARRANTY
1605
HOMESTEAD'S
HILLSIDE DODGE
HILLSIDE
DODGE
HELP KEEP THE
NEW PITTSBURGH
CLEAN
PLACE
LITTER HERE

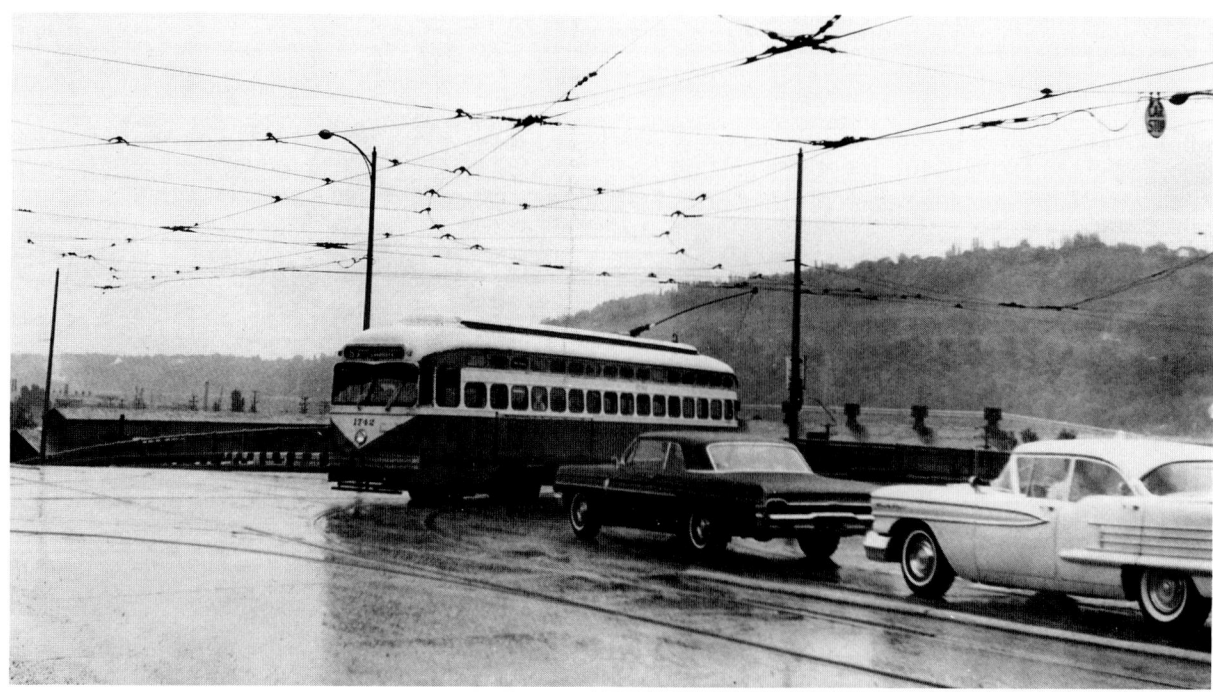

OPPOSITE PAGE, TOP:
On May 19, 1963, the 67-SWISSVALE RANKIN BRADDOCK line had a billboard car assigned to its route. Painted dark blue with orange lettering, No. 1605 heads outbound on 4th Avenue at Smithfield Street. The Dodges may have had a five year warranty, but the trolley car was in its 18th year of service with well over half a million miles behind it.

OPPOSITE PAGE, BOTTOM:
Having climbed up from Talbot Avenue, inbound No. 1742 turns left through the rain onto Braddock Avenue in Rankin.

THIS PAGE, TOP:
In a fine example of retaining streetcar service and incorporating it into modern highway construction, the Rankin bridge complex handled routes 55 and 67. No. 1759 is inbound on Braddock Avenue.

THIS PAGE, SIDE:
No. 1797 has made the loop at the end of the 67-SWISSVALE RANKIN BRADDOCK line and faces inbound on June 7, 1964. The mill is Carnegie-Illinois Steel Company's.

OPPOSITE PAGE:
76-HAMILTON ran from downtown to Wilkinsburg by way of Fifth Avenue. The service stop here is at Bellefield Avenue in Oakland. The luxurious Hotel Webster Hall and the spires of a beautiful church form a delightful urban backdrop. No. 1485 is inbound on May 18, 1963.

THIS PAGE, TOP:
During baseball games at Forbes Field and football games at Pitt Stadium, special cars signed STADIUM-FORBES FIELD were dispatched to carry the crowds. The cars laid over during the game here at the site of the former Duquesne car house just off Fifth Avenue between Neville and Craig Avenues.

THIS PAGE, BOTTOM:
The camera finds inbound No. 1433 making the transition from center of the street running where Wood Street is one way to double track running as Wood Street becomes bi-directional. The intersection is with Penn Street in Wilkinsburg. Outbound route 76 and 87 cars made the left turn here.

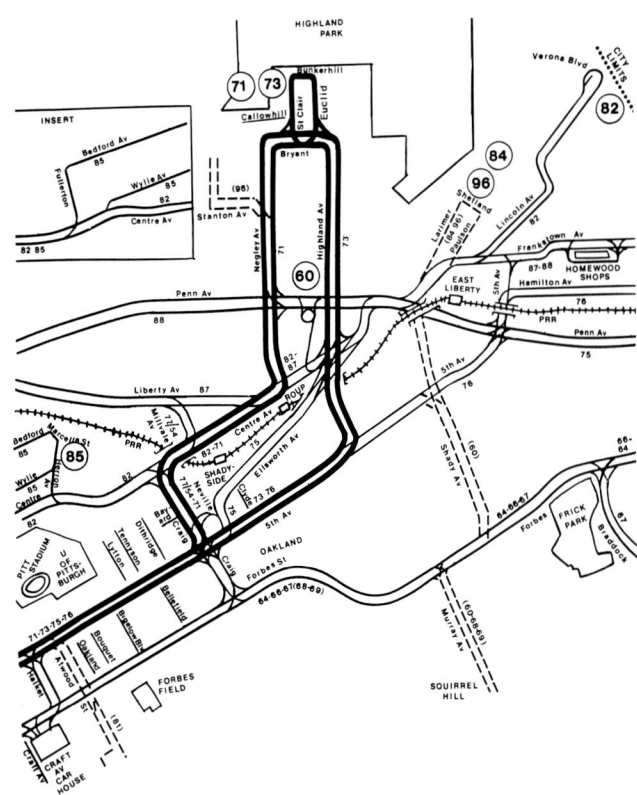

MAP:
This map of the Oakland and East Liberty areas happens to highlight routes 71-NEGLEY HIGHLAND PARK and 73-HIGHLAND. Both routes served Highland Park, one of many parks in Pittsburgh's extensive park system, and both came out of downtown by way of Fifth Avenue.

BOTTOM, LEFT:
Bantering between the motorman and boys on vacation takes place beneath the sycamore trees on St. Clair Street. Highland Park rises in the far background behind No. 1559 at this layover point for route 71. Negley Avenue was named for an early Swiss settler in this area.

BOTTOM, RIGHT:
A better glimpse of the park is seen here on Bunkerhill Street as No. 1603 approaches St. Clair. A playground with tennis courts lies to the right of the picture.

TOP:
Between 1926 and 1928, the University of Pittsburgh built its magnificent 35-story Cathedral of Learning, or "inverted mine shaft" as its collegiate football rivals called it. It is seen from Fifth Avenue behind No. 1730 maintaining the 75-WILKINSBURG via EAST LIBERTY outbound schedule on June 6, 1964.

BOTTOM:
No. 1475 lays over on a siding in middle of Hay Street. This was the Wilkinsburg terminal of route 75. The embankment in the background carries the Pennsylvania Railroad's main line. Its Wilkinsburg station is a block away to the left of the picture. The Pennsy's local commuter service had ended by June, 1966 when this picture was taken. The trolley line was to last barely six months more.

TOP:
No. 1728 cruises inbound on 73-HIGHLAND, passing through University of Pittsburgh territory on June 4, 1966. The cross street is Oakland, with Pitt Stadium a short walk to the left.

BOTTOM:
Another all street-running route on the East End was 88-FRANKSTOWN which came out to East Liberty from the downtown area over Penn Avenue. On Frankstown Avenue, the cars passed Pittsburgh Railway's Homewood shops and ended their runs just short of the city limits. Trolleys on 76-HAMILTON operate on the Tioga Street trackage in the foreground. Cars on 87-ARDMORE operate on the Oakwood Street tracks behind No. 1511. Those tracks join, and both of the other routes continue into the Boro of Wilkinsburg.

The three-way intersection of Center, Ellsworth, and Highland Avenues in East Liberty was last three-way trolley intersection in the United States. Not that there were that many, however, because the street configuration is itself unusual. Even in this case, Center and Ellsworth Avenues join immediately to the left of these views. It is also remarkable that all of the lines were double-tracked and, as was usual for the engineering layout of Pittsburgh Railways, there were normally unused connecting tracks between the lines. This provided a high degree of operating flexibility.

The vantage point of this series of views is the northeast corner of the intersection looking southwest onto Ellsworth Avenue in the left center background. It was May 20, 1963, one of Pittsburgh's many umbrella days.

TOP:
The traction action begins with No. 1523 heading outbound on 75-WILKINSBURG via EAST LIBERTY. It has pulled away from the line of automobiles behind it on Ellsworth.

MIDDLE:
Outbound on 87-ARDMORE, No. 1509 enters from the right. This is Center Avenue whose tracks were shared with the 82-LINCOLN line.

BOTTOM:
Also outbound, No. 1466 splashes across the intersection on the South Highland Avenue portion of its run on 73-HIGHLAND.

MAP:
The 87-ARDMORE line was ambitious in terms of its length, running as it did from downtown through East Liberty, Homewood, Wilkinsburg, Forest Hills, East Pittsburgh, and Turtle Creek to reach its destination in Wilmerding. The line's name derives from the boulevard through Forest Hills.

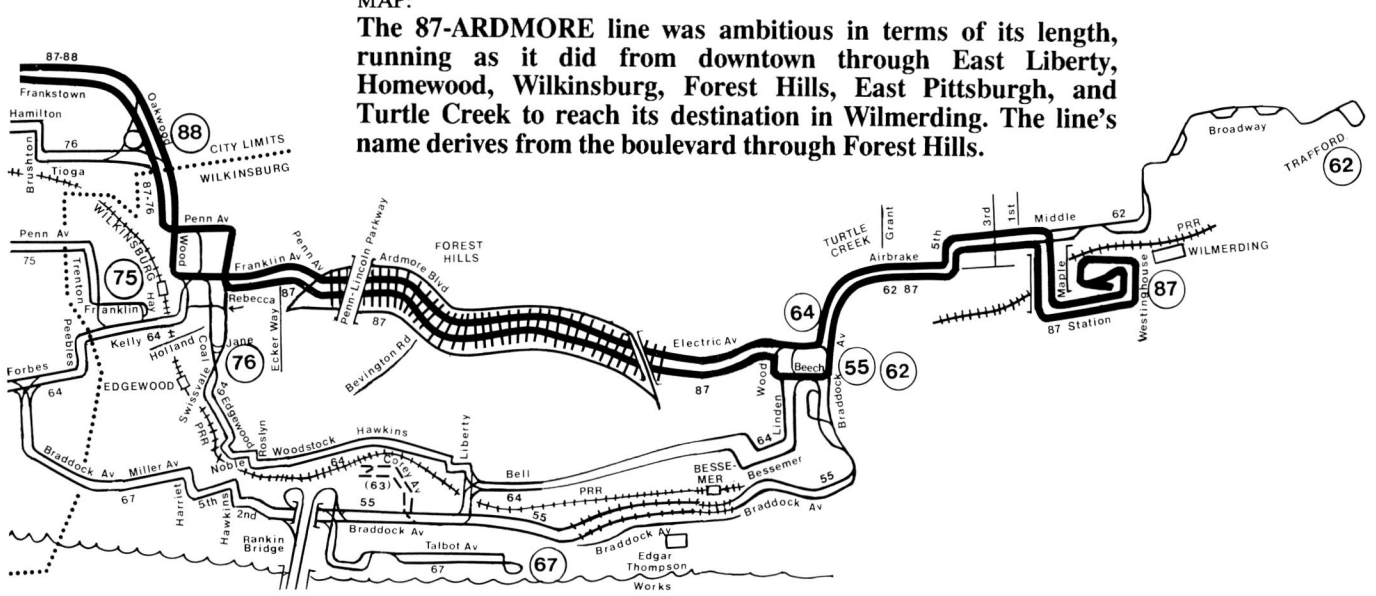

OPPOSITE PAGE:
The 87-ARDMORE line crosses the extensive Pennsylvania Railroad trackage in Wilmerding on the Maple Avenue bridge. No. 1550 rounds a curve in the bridge alignment.

THIS PAGE:
After miles of laborious street running, No. 1525 springs out onto private right of way beyond Wilkinsburg. The trolley is outbound and has just passed under the graceful arches of the Penn-Lincoln Parkway. US 30 West joins US 22 and I-376 here, reaching downtown in eight miles and a matter of a few minutes through the Squirrel Hill tunnel. The trolley's route was more roundabout, more congested, and much more time consuming.

TOP:
At running speed, it was a bumpy ride down Ardmore Boulevard's center of the road right of way. Signals protected No. 1525 as it moved outbound on this steady downgrade to East Pittsburgh. The boulevard is US 30 in this section through Forest Hills, named after the community in the New York City borough of Queens which hosts the world championship tennis matches.

BOTTOM:
US 30, the Lincoln Highway, sweeps overhead as the center right of way drops down, following the contour of the land. A short S-turn puts the tracks and No. 1513 right in the middle of Electric Avenue.

TOP:
Principal thoroughfare in the town of Turtle Creek is Air Brake Avenue. Even so, parked automobiles had to infringe a bit on pedestrians in order to clear the trolleys. No. 1525 is outbound on June 5, 1966.

BOTTOM:
Outbound nearing Wilmerding, No. 1543 crests the hill on Middle Avenue at 1st Street. Not only is this a no passing zone, it is also obviously a no parking zone on both sides of the street!

TOP:
Outbound in 1966, No. 1550 tip toes off of Middle Avenue onto the Maple Avenue bridge. Until 1962, this intersection was a junction with the 62-TRAFFORD line. Trafford was the connecting point with West Penn Railways' network of trolleys in southwestern Pennsylvania. Route 62 was a side of the road operation with frequent passing sidings, remnants of the days when trolley freight cars of West Penn operated through to Pittsburgh. Freight service ended in 1941 and West Penn abandoned its link at Trafford in 1942.

BOTTOM:
No. 1537 outbound on 87-ARDMORE nears its Wilmerding terminal.

This overall view at Wilmerding looks east on June 27, 1965. The Pennsylvania Railroad's Wilmerding station is located at the curve of its main line tracks. The station platform separates the leftmost track from the four tracks at the curve. Access to the station was beneath the tracks. Car No. 1537 reaches the Wilmerding loop traveling westward, the result of a spiral route off the Maple Avenue bridge, east on Station Street, north on Westinghouse Street to the railroad, then west to the 87-ARDMORE terminal. The terminal had a short spur track for emergency car storage.

THE SOUTH SIDE

OPPOSITE PAGE:
The Pennsylvania Railroad's Smithfield Street station is now abandoned, but on June 7, 1964 the public could stand there and see this scene. The view faces toward the Smithfield Street bridge over which No. 1621 has crossed on its outbound run on 50-CARSON STREET. The impressive building on the left is the Pittsburgh & Lake Erie Railroad's station, now the site of the Station Square Shopping Mall.

MAP:
The dramatic heights overlooking the Golden Triangle and downtown area are served by 40-MT. WASHINGTON. The line was another of the imperatives on the itinerary of every railfan, and a tour of route 40 was often combined with a ride on one of the inclines.

BOTTOM:
This view of downtown Pittsburgh was taken as cars on the now-abandoned Castle Shannon Incline were about to pass. The base station was at Carson Street and Arlington Avenue.

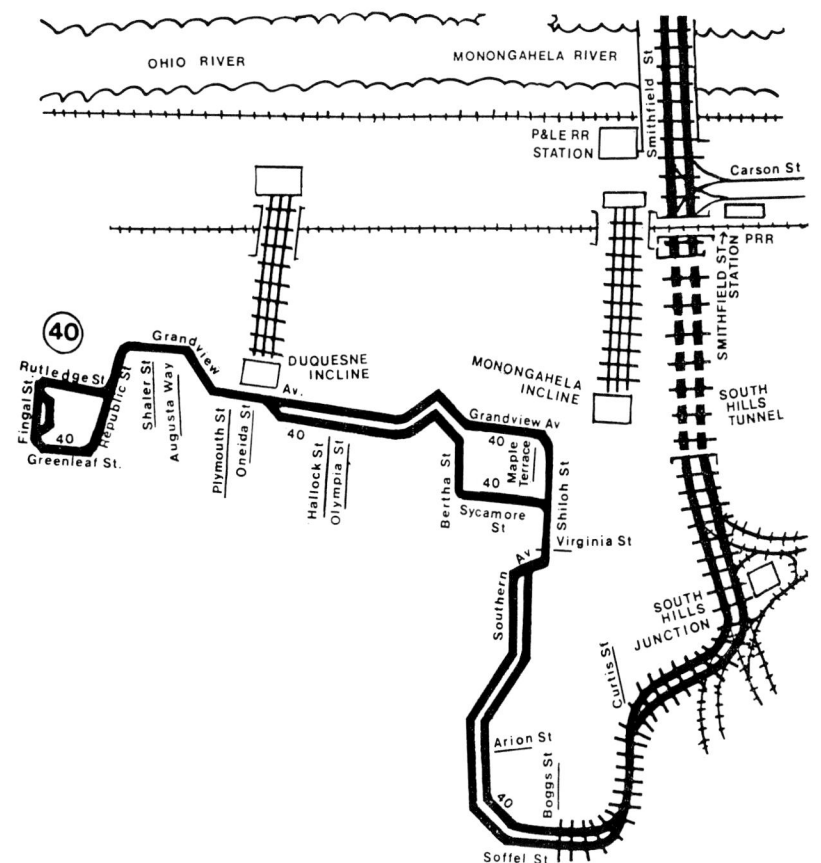

69

TOP:
Trolleys on 40-MT. WASHINGTON tunnel through the cliffs along the river and attack the heights from the South Side. The first part of the ascent is on private right of way which ends by bursting out onto Soffel Street here at Boggs. Ladies with shopping bags and packages have alighted from No. 1636. One of them waits for the outbound car to pass before crossing the street.

BOTTOM:
On June 6, 1966, the motorman of No. 1638 looked in vain for the driver who parked his car too close to the corner. If the trolley were to proceed with its turn onto Shiloh Street from Sycamore, the rear would swing out and hit the side of the automobile. Because this proved to be a lengthy delay, block tickets were issued to inbound passengers for use on the Monongahela Incline two blocks away.

TOP:
White lines were painted on the streets to indicate the street space that must be allowed for passing trolleys. The lines swing wide at corners as illustrated on Sycamore Street as No. 1663 negotiates the turn from Bertha Street.

MIDDLE:
The milkman's Divco Twin, a drive-it-standing-up delivery truck, is parked at summit station of the Duquesne Incline. No. 1672 moves inbound off of one of the three sections of single track on 40-MT. WASHINGTON.

BOTTOM:
Looking down the Duquesne Incline one sees the Ohio River, tracks of the Pittsburgh & Lake Erie Railroad, and rooftop advertising.

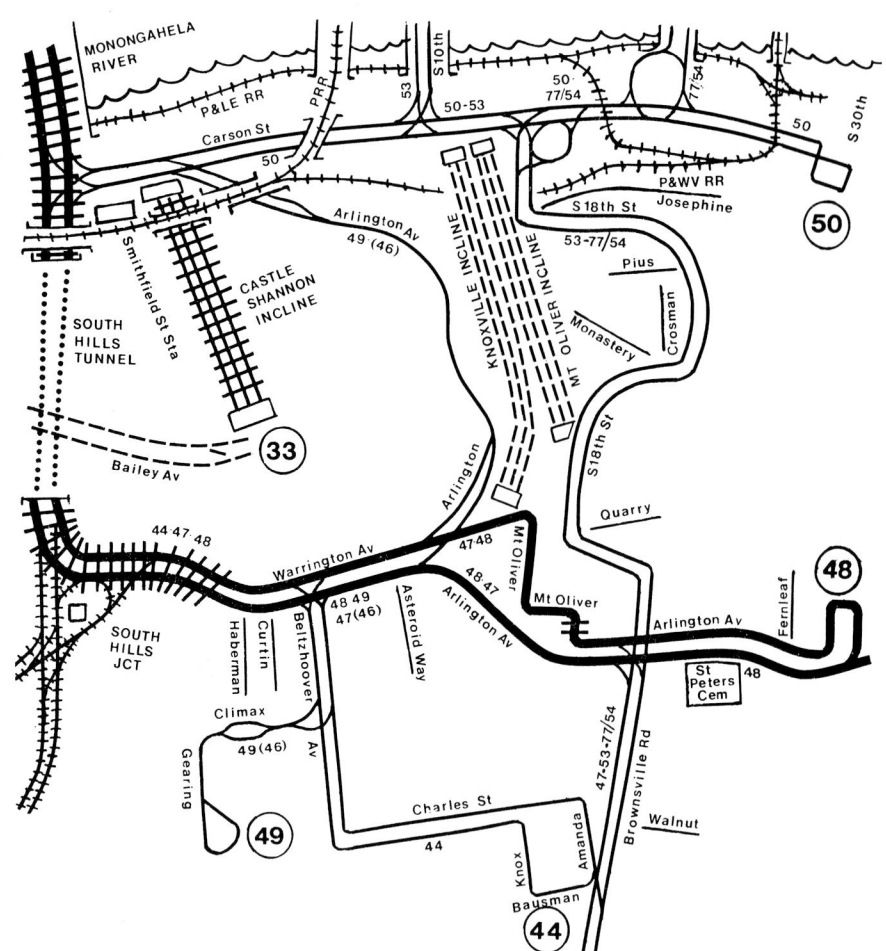

MAP:
Railroads, trolleys, and inclines fill the South Side transportation map. The dramatic changes in elevation are implied by the inclines, but the topography also inflicts a roller coaster-like profile on the lines across the South Hills.

Before the days of the loop at the outer end of the 48-ARLINGTON line, double-ended trolley cars switched back in the middle of the street. The track in the extreme left foreground is a remnant of that means of operation. No. 1672 waits it time to leave the loop on June 9, 1964.

TOP:
No. 1655 hums uphill on Arlington Avenue as it twists past Greenleaf Street. The trolley wears the winged dash emblem typically found on PCC cars over the paint job that gave them good visibility. In the bottom picture, the trolley has the so-called "V-front" paint job with the dash emblem removed.

Having come upgrade, No. 1657 starts downgrade. The location is St. Peter's Cemetery on Arlington Avenue, not far from the terminus of the 48-ARLINGTON line. The trolley is outbound through a pleasant residential community.

OPPOSITE PAGE:
The inbound track of the 48-ARLINGTON line made a short transition between Arlington Avenue and Mount Oliver Street. The move was made in a residential district on a private right of way close to a house. It was perhaps the ultimate in backyard railroading, at least until March of 1968 when trolley service ended. No. 1657 enters the unusual trackage.

THIS PAGE:
No. 1652, inbound on 48-ARLINGTON, rolls past the point on Warrington Avenue where the summit station of the Knoxville Incline was once located. On June 28, 1965, an Atlantic gasoline station occupied the site; today it is the site of a convenience store.

TOP:
The Mt. Oliver section was served by 44-KNOXVILLE & PA STA. On June 4, 1964, billboard car No. 1623 advertised the 1964 Plymouth for the Allegheny County Chrysler dealers. Even then, Chrysler offered long-term, high-mileage warranties. The trolley is seen turning from Bausman onto Amanda, near the terminal of the line.

BOTTOM:
The car has reached the layover point of route 44, this safety island on Amanda and Charles Street.

TOP:
Gas was 24.9 cents per gallon on June 9, 1964 when this photograph was taken of No. 1669 running on the 53-CARRICK line. The line of travel is inbound on Brownsville Road at Arlington Avenue where route 53 crossed route 48.

BOTTOM:
No. 1663 tilts down an 8% grade on South 18th Street at Monastery Place. This is an inbound trip on 53-CARRICK.

OPPOSITE PAGE:
One of the surviving lines from Pittsburgh's trolley era is the much-changed "Over the hill" route on Arlington Avenue. Originally the 46-BROWNSVILLE line, it became 49-BELTZHOOVER at the end of September, 1946. In 1971, routes 48 and 49 were combined into 49-ARLINGTON-WARRINGTON which was renumbered as route 52 in 1984. The line was originally double tracked, then single tracked, then rebuilt for the new Light Rail System.

In this 1963 view, car 1642 climbs Arlington Avenue on the 49-BELTZHOOVER line. It swings left in traffic, moving onto the single track portion of the route. The overpass in the background carries the Pennsylvania Railroad tracks to the Panhandle bridge. The sloping landmark above and to the left of the overpass is the Monongahela Incline.

THIS PAGE:
No. 1736 prepares to turn right off of Beltzhoover Avenue onto Warrington Avenue. On its inbound run on 49-BELTZHOOVER, the car has operated over single track on Climax and Gearing Streets.

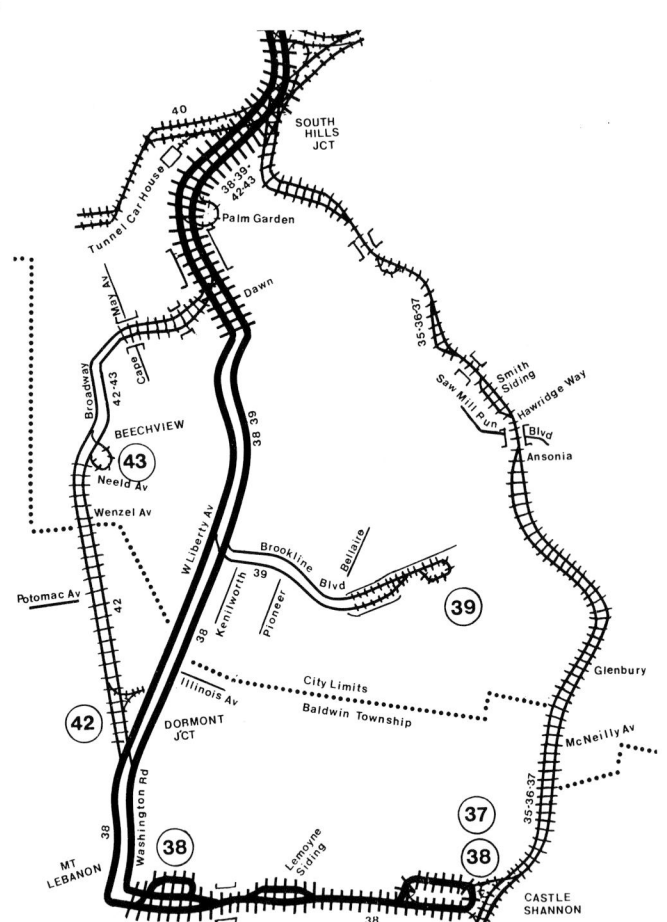

MAP:
A vast amount of trackage on the South Side was interesting because long sections of its private right of way cut through areas on its own, rather than being at roadside. Trolleys using the former interurban lines to Charleroi and Washington made excellent time out of the city by using the South Hills tunnel and private right of way. The tunnel and these rights of way preserved the viability of rail service in the area until modernized and developed as a light rail system.

TOP, RIGHT:
Tracks of the 38-MT. LEBANON and 39-BROOKLINE lines joined those of 42-DORMONT and 43-NEELD AVENUE at a point called Dawn. No. 1640 inbound on route 39 climbs a ramp to reach the junction.

BOTTOM:
Inbound No. 1633 reaches the junction on private right of way from its trip over Broadway in the Beechview section. Its route was designated 42/38-MT. LEBANON BEECHVIEW, a combination of route 42 and the outer end of route 38.

TOP:
Outbound on 39-BROOKLINE, No. 1654 reaches the bottom of the track ramp from the junction at Dawn. The car is about to enter West Liberty Avenue. When this ramp opened in 1939, it was one of the earliest traffic grade separations in the city. When 39-BROOKLINE cars ceased running in 1966, the ramp was closed but today it is part of the South PATway.

Inbound from the junction at Dawn, this trestle carried trolleys toward South Hills Junction. No. 1234 approaches the north end of the trestle where there was a stop called Palm Garden, named for a turn of the century dance hall. As part of the South PATway project, a parallel bridge was built to carry both buses and trolleys across the valley. *Photograph by Richard Anderson.*

The 38-MT. LEBANON line had only six more days as an independent route when this picture was taken on May 19, 1963. On May 25th, the line was combined with 42-DORMONT. No. 1650 has picked up an inbound fare at the safety island on West Liberty and Illinois Avenues. The trolley is still within the borough of Dormont, whose businesses line its main thoroughfare.

TOP:
Dormont Junction at West Liberty and McFarland is the location of this view of No. 1619 working inbound on 38-MT. LEBANON.

BOTTOM:
By 1965, No. 1619 had been fitted with a roof headlight and a pilot, accoutrements appropriate for the open running on the SHANNON-LIBRARY line. Its dash lights were retained. The 45-JEFFERSON bus at left connected Castle Shannon with Mt. Lebanon.

RENAISSANCE OF THE SEVENTIES

Starting in 1972, a startling turn of events took place: the trolley system that had been in a steady decline in the sixties took a sudden turn upward. Incredibly shabby trolleys began to bloom in fresh paint jobs in a bright bouquet of colors.

On June 22, 1972, Harold H. Geissenheimer, assistant director of transit operations, was named to succeed John W. Dameron as director of transit operations by John T. Mauro, executive director of the Port Authority of Allegheny County.

Mr. Geissenheimer, with 22 years of transit experience at the time of the appointment, joined PAT in 1964 as a transit engineer and was soon appointed director of planning, serving six years in that position. He had been acting manager for a short period prior to becoming assistant director of transit operations in 1970.

Mr. Geissenheimer has since left to work for the Chicago Transit Authority, and later for the Municipal Railway of San Francisco. He now does consulting work in New Jersey, but before he left he instituted a program of rehabilitation. The program included spectacular graphics which focused Pittsburghers' attention on their transit system. This focus made it possible for the remaining trolley lines to remain in service. It also helped pave the way for the modern light-rail system of the eighties, including the Pittsburgh subway which had been the city's dream since 1912.

On July 26, 1972, car 1730 emerged from the paint shop in a psychedelic sunburst paint scheme of red, orange and yellow, with the word "trolley," in fancy script on its sides. This graphic was so unique that a photo of the car—in black and white, of course—appeared in the *New York Times*.

The painting of "color dynamic" cars continued, transforming each such car with a new color scheme of vertical bands in one of a series of colors on the front and rear third with a white center section. In addition, more "Spectaculars" appeared, reinstating the Pittsburgh Railways policy of total repainting that had produced its billboard cars. By the eighties, PAT once again decided to go with a single red and white paint scheme, but in the seventies, the "billboard" cars were quite numerous and became even more spectacular and whimsical than those of the sixties. Some of the more unusual repaints included the magenta-white-magenta 1734 which carried the slogan "The Jolly Trolley"—ironic since former director Dameron often referred to those interested in keeping trolley service as "trolley jollies." Perhaps there was a bit of satire in this.

The victory of the Pittsburgh Steelers football team in Super Bowl XIV inspired "The Terrible Trolley," a menacing vision in black and yellow applied to No. 1713 and looking like a rolling Darth Vader. But by far the most bizarre was "Clipper Ship" car 1794, formerly No. 1669. It was transformed into a mock-up of a sightseeing boat, complete with life preservers and fake smokestacks. The stacks increased the height of the car so much that the car had to operate via the over-the-hill 49 line. It could not make clearances in the South Hills Tunnel, the ceiling of which had been lowered to accommodate ventilating equipment intended to clear the exhaust of diesel buses.

In 1984, the Gateway Center leg of the subway opened and replaced all surface trolley operation in downtown Pittsburgh. A brand-new terminal and shop have been built at the South Hills Village shopping mall complex in Bethel Park. The new trolley facilities replaced Tunnel car house and shop at the southern end of the South Hills Tunnel. The 42/38 line, including the old 38-A shuttle line from Clearview loop in Mt. Lebanon to Castle Shannon has been totally rebuilt and double-tracked from Washington Junction to Dorchester Junction. A new branch built off the line at that point runs to South Hills Village.

The first of the new Siemens-DuWag articulated light rail vehicles have gone into service. Forty-five of the all-electric PCC cars were to have been totally rebuilt to supplement them. However, budget limitations and some technical difficulties halted the project after only 16 were completed.

The routes have all been renumbered and the track layout at South Hills Junction has been changed. The familiar old brick administration building, seemingly there since the year One, has been demolished.

Larry Lovejoy, speaking at the Electric Railroader's Association banquet in Pittsburgh in 1982, said that when the Siemens Company received specifications for the new LRVs that called for them to be able to negotiate a ten percent grade, they asked if, through an error, a decimal point had been misplaced and that maybe it should have been a 1.0% grade. A look at the topography of Pittsburgh would have rendered such a question unnecessary.

The following is a chronology of events starting with the debut of the first "color dynamic" car in 1972 and continuing into the 1980s:

May, 1972: No. 1767 became the first car to be painted in the new vertical-stripe color scheme. It was orange-white-orange.

July 26, 1972: PAT staged a parade through downtown, featuring the new "mod" paint schemes on No. 1767 in orange, 1744 in yellow, 1762 in red, and 1730 in a mod desire psychedelic color scheme.

Aug. 1, 1972: rush-hour express service was instituted on the LIBRARY line.

Nov. 8, 1972: No. 1616, the first 1600-series car to be rehabilitated, emerged from the shop as the red, white and blue No. 1776—"THE SPIRIT OF '76".

Nov. 18, 1973: work began on the reconstruction of the South Hills tunnel to enable it to accommodate buses as well as trolleys. One track at a time was taken out of service to be worked on and the 49-ARLINGTON WARRINGTON line was used as a detour route on weekends when the tunnel was closed for this major reconstruction.

1974: No. 1647 became No. 1779, an orange-white-orange car that was the first of the experimental "double-enders." The double-ending, applied to three cars, consisted of a trolley pole on each end and a headlight over the rear window. Rear-end operation was accomplished with a back-up controller behind the rear seat. The experimental installation was seldom used and has since been removed from all three cars. No. 1779 had its extra equipment removed in early 1976 when it got a new front end and was renumbered 1976. No. 1781, a yellow-white-yellow car, returned to single-end status in early 1977. The third double-ender was No. 1780, in red-white-red; it became a single-ender in late 1977. These double-end cars were not popular with the operators, as operating from the rear end meant having to sit sideways in the rear seat, which was uncomfortable for any appreciable distance. They were double-ended originally to make them more flexible in case any line was blocked by landslide or other obstruction. The new LRVs are double-ended.

Sept. 1974: The Transportation Systems center for the urban Mass Transit Administration completed its report on "Skybus." This unorthodox means of transit had been proposed as a replacement for rail transit on the South Side lines when announced in 1969. The report stated that "the use of vehicles without attendants has not been demonstrated in line-haul revenue service to date.". It went on to state that the system, "from the standpoint of adequate safety, availability and social acceptability has not been demonstrated with sufficient quantitative analyses or experience with existing transit systems." This report doomed the Skybus just in time to save the Drake line from a bus replacement while the Skybus could be built on its right of way. Critics of the Skybus system also pointed out that a workable switch had not been developed and that it was incompatible with existing transit facilities, thus limiting its flexibility

July 4, 1975: South Hills tunnel was re-opened for two-way trolley service on weekends and holidays, No. 1639 was transformed from its shabby appearance as it emerged from its cocoon as No. 1788—the BICENTENNIAL TOUR TROLLEY. Hourly service on routes 35 and 36 was shortened to 40-minute headways.

Oct. 26, 1975: full trolley service was restored through the tunnel, ending detour service over the hill on the 49 line.

February 23, 1976: Harold E. Geissenheimer resigned from the Port Authority to take a post with the Chicago Transit Authority as general operations manager.

July 4, 1976: Low-floor car 3756, on loan from the Arden Trolley Museum, ran in the downtown area as part of the Bicentennial Independence Day celebration.

February 10, 1978: a collision between trolley No. 1790 and a bus on the South PATway killed the bus driver and four bus passengers.

July, 1981: No. 4000, the first of 45 remanufactured PCC cars, built using salvaged components from old PCC cars, began its test runs.

July 3, 1985: free rides were given to the public in the newly-completed subway, between Gateway Center and Station Square stations, after a ribbon-cutting ceremony, officially dedicating the new facility.

July 7, 1985: the last trolleys run on the street downtown in the wee hours of the morning as all service after that is routed via the Panhandle Bridge into the new subway.

TOP:
In all its psychedelic glory, No. 1730 dreams its way through South Hills Junction on a sunny day in late May, 1980. The red, orange, and yellow paint scheme was "Mod Desire." The car was later repainted in the PAT design of three vertical stripes.

BOTTOM:
The "Clipper Ship" lays over on the South Hills Junction loop on May 21, 1978. This fanciful car was made in an effort to promote Pittsburgh tourism. It is said that two more cars were considered for similar projects, but this was to be the only total makeover. It ran for a few years, but by 1980 it had been put into storage.

TOP:
In 1966, testing took the form of a run by the Westinghouse Air Brake Company's test car on the Library line. The operator has stopped at Glenbury to make a time check at the headway recorder box en route to the test site was at Kings School. This location is now the southern end of the joint trolley and bus PATway. The frame building at right housed a grocery store, but fell victim to the need for an off-ramp.

BOTTOM:
In 1985, testing took the form of exercising the new Siemens/DuWag equipment. The train swoops down off the Panhandle bridge toward the stop at Station Square on the south side of the Monongahela River.

Ron Beal

THE ARDEN MUSEUM

The Arden Trolley Museum is operated by the Pennsylvania Railway Museum Association, a non-profit historical and educational organization. The association's focus is on transportation history.

In addition to offering trolley rides over the right of way of Pittsburgh Railways' old interurban line to Washington, museum members maintain a library and publish books and articles. Included in the thousands of visitors each year are groups of school children who are given rides on the historic equipment.

The museum's trolley collection includes historic equipment from Pittsburgh, Johnstown, Philadelphia, and New Orleans.

New members are welcome in both active and associate membership. Active members can qualify to operate the cars. Any member can participate by giving tours, staffing the gift shop, helping to restore and maintain the trolley collection, build track and overhead, as well as publicize the museum and help it to raise funds. Many associate members live in other parts of the country and give their support through membership dues.

Membership benefits include fantrips, receipt of the bi-monthly publication TROLLEY FARE, and discounts at the museum gift shop. Regular monthly meetings are held on the second Thursday.

THIS PAGE:
Low-floor Pittsburgh Railways No. 3756 poses at the Arden Trolley Museum. Built in 1925, this car was one of 20 high-speed cars intended for semi-interurban use. It is also one of nine to be equipped with a door on its left side for use on the 23-CORAOPOLIS-SEWICKLEY line in order to avoid having passengers alight on a busy highway at many of its car stops.

OPPOSITE PAGE MAP:
By 1961, most of Pittsburgh's trolley network was intact. As indicated, most lines already abandoned were at the periphery of the system.